BREATHE CONSCIOUSLY
and be happy!

BREATHE CONSCIOUSLY
and be happy!

the breath which turned my whole life

INGA KORYAGINA

BALBOA.
PRESS
A DIVISION OF HAY HOUSE

Balboa Press books may be ordered through booksellers or by contacting:

Balboa Press
A Division of Hay House
1663 Liberty Drive
Bloomington, IN 47403
www.balboapress.com
1-(877) 407-4847

ISBN: 978-1-4525-3535-7 (e)
ISBN: 978-1-4525-3533-3 (sc)

Printed in the United States of America

Balboa Press rev. date: 2/07/2012

THE INTRODUCTION

THE FIRST BREATH

My first experience with rebirthing breathwork techniques happened in 1998. That August, the country was in crisis and I remember prices increasing steadily in the stores. But fortunately we didn't dwell on them thanks to the protection that our subconsciousness has over the psyche. People carried on with their own lives and the government did the same. I continued to live as well, working harder and harder without seeing a ray of hope. I was completely subdued by my responsibility for the small amount of money my family had, or should I say, by the lack of it. I stopped smiling and fell into depression, but at that time I didn't even realize it. Besides, who cares about just one person when an entire country is being ruined?

And then, absolutely unexpectedly, as always, I was told about a training that could help solve my internal problems. I didn't care about how it could help me; my main concern was to do something to get out of my hopeless position. Therefore I took part in the training. The training was led by a team of young people who had learned some breathwork techniques in India and brought their experience to Russia. They didn't teach us, but within four days' training, we were able to look inside ourselves and discover something new. I knew

I was there to learn about meditation and rebirthing breathwork, but the team didn't attempt to teach us, and they didn't explain the training. The group was rather large. There were about five or six trainers and thirty participants—just small enough that each client was supported psychologically by a trainer. The first time I meditated, I suddenly saw myself as Buddha, and, without understanding what was going on and what I should do, I became frightened that I would have to live in a monastery. This was the first time I encountered spirituality, and it was very difficult to accept.

Once we entered a hall that was covered with rugs. Some loud music started playing and we were told just to lie down, close our eyes, and breathe. We weren't told how we should breathe, why we were breathing, or what would happen next. And I started to breathe. My body was turning inside out and twisting from inside to outside. I was screaming and shouting, groaning and sobbing violently. It seemed to me that it would never come to an end. I had an impression that my sufferings lasted about four hours, although it was only an hour.

Only a few years later, I found out that what I was attempting was called rebirthing, which is a special breath technique. It is as old as the hills and is a technique that uses the breath to pull the body out, to realize moral traumas it has been suffering from since the moment of conception. Yes, just like I said, from the very moment of conception, because parents' thoughts contribute to each child's mission of a future little baby, his purpose and aims.

Coming back to my first rebirthing experience, I can tell that it changed my whole life. For the first time, I was able to tell people around me that I was divorced and my daughter was already nine years old. When I told this to my colleagues, with whom I had been working for three years already, they were in shock. The divorce, which I went through when I was 19, wasn't really a divorce in the usual sense. I was simply thrown out with the child on the street, just like a dog. The experience left me emotionally frozen for almost ten years. I constantly had this picture in front of my eyes: I come home from the hospital and my husband slightly opens the door, just as much as the chain lets him, and says that if I try to enter, he will let the dog loose. That chain was constantly pursuing me. After such a traumatic event, I had no hope of a family life. But exactly in that moment, my spiritual searches and my path to God began.

Approximately three years later after my first breath training, when I was already practicing the Reiki system of natural healing, I went to another training which was explicitly called rebirthing. At this training, I realized what had happened to me during that initial training in 1998. A hearty thanks to Uliana Tsoy, my Reiki master; she explained everything and made comments on what was happening to us. All my rebirthing sessions were physically painful. There were always the same symptoms, and I was convinced that rebirthing was a very difficult physical activity. We were breathing with an open mouth. Skipping forward, I will say that it is one of the most powerful types of breath, intended for revealing and transforming very difficult problems. This type of breath is also called holotropic breathwork and is carried out in a group or in pairs. When I myself became a Reiki teacher in 2005 and acquired the right to teach rebirthing in 2006, I continued to train and carry out breathing sessions with an open mouth. I was quite surprised, having traveled to America to study with Leonardo Orr, a rebirthing pioneer, to learn during my first session that rebirthing is a conscious breathing technique and is done very softly through the nose, without any physical twisting, and, moreover, is strictly carried out individually. When I tried to breathe that way, I fell in love with rebirthing at once and stopped considering it difficult or painful. Now I can breathe easily whenever I want and, most importantly, I derive great pleasure from it!

I have decided to write this book about the simplicity and efficiency of this breathing technique its transformative power. Before the trip I was asking myself: what other way can my subconscious surprise me? I decided to take part in the Orr's rebirthing seminars not only to relive my own experiences, but to learn the breathwork technique from the pioneer of rebirthing. I couldn't have known then what was concealed inside me and what kind of transformations would occur! I also didn't expect to unlock my internal healer. But it happened; I became a healer and I'm eager to share this gift with my dear clients and readers!

INHALE + EXHALE = BREATH CYCLE!

Those who practice yoga may say that there is no difference between the yoga breath and rebirthing breathwork, as it is technically difficult to invent anything new in a breath. Actually, the difference is in the magic of healing from the tension of life problems that occur due to duration (a breathwork session lasts for an hour) and position (the person is lying down during an hour session). There is a lot to say and to write about the advantages of breathwork, but unless the person tries it himself, these advantages mean nothing. Therefore, I describe the types of breath exercises that I was taught during Orr's trainings, which you can also find in all Leonardo Orr's books. Each exercise takes 3-5 seconds: together they should last 3-5 minutes.

Types of breathwork exercises:

I. "Twenty cycles." Twenty breathwork cycles (INHALE + EXHALE = a cycle) through the nose of different durations: after four short inhale-exhales, take one deep and long inhale-exhale. Repeat this sequence four times without breaks.

It is important that all twenty respiratory cycles go together and merge into one breathwork sequence, similar to one continuous inhale-exhale. With each short inhale, it is necessary to try to fill all the possible space in yourself, and with each exhalation, you must let out all the air from your lungs until they are completely empty. Don't keep air inside; exhale it at once. Breathing should be smooth and free, it is not necessary to force or control it. If you breathe correctly, you'll feel how, not only air, but also energy, spreads through a body. This is called the *conscious power breath* or *energy of the conscious breath*. During a breath it is possible to limit a stream of energy, and it is possible to limit a stream of air during energy inhalation. If you haven't practiced similar breathing before, don't do this exercise more often than once a week, otherwise you will unleash a lot of intense experiences out of your subconsciousness and you will urgently have to consult the psychotherapist or look for a rebirther.

II. "Tongue behind teeth." Twenty connected respiratory cycles with a small addition—at breath, it is necessary to hold the tongue clamped between the teeth constantly. Lips are closed, the tongue is pushed between the teeth and lifted upward for an upper lip or pushed downward under a lower lip. Do twenty respiratory cycles through the nose. You will notice how your sensations change.

This exercise is useful for those who grit their teeth while sleeping, sleep uneasily, or are often angry. It can be practiced before sleep, in bed, or when you are angry. Breathe directly on the object of your irritation, and it will instantly disappear! You will learn to supervise yourself better. By opening your teeth, you will relax completely.

III. "Breathing with an open mouth." Twenty connected respiratory cycles, but not through the nose—through the mouth. Open the mouth as is wide as it is convenient (for the duration of the exercise), inhale four short breaths followed by one long exhalation, and then repeat this combination four times. During this exercise, weaken the tongue, consciously pull in air and let out, and also observe your sensations. Breathing through the mouth is valuable because it is possible to absolutely liberate your blocked energy and repressed feelings. If you have unpleasant sensations, return to nasal breathing to work on the problems more effectively.

Proceeding from my own breath experience, I can say that breathing through the mouth is a more powerful tool for bringing up deep problems, which don't want to rise to consciousness by themselves. There is a feeling of stagnation. With the help of this breathing technique, you won't be bogged down any more. It's better to practiced this with a rebirther—you'll get everything out of your subconsciousness pretty quickly and won't even be able to understand what it is. However, as breathing through the mouth loosens the vegetation system of the body and makes it very sensitive, your mood may worsen and you may encounter all the fears you've forgotten for a long time. Nasal breathing is salutary itself, but don't hope that it will cure you right after the first exercise—the real effect comes after several eight-hour sessions, and only under the guidance of a rebirther.

IV. "Breathing through the nose with an open mouth." Twenty connected respiratory cycles through the nose with a widely opened mouth—this makes the breath soundless. This type of breath demands certain skills, but offers all the advantages of both nasal and oral breathing. After a while, you will notice that this technique develops intuition and is the most effective way to get rid of negative energy in a body.

V. "Silent energy breathing." The main feature of this breathing lies in a soft inhalation and an exhalation—air, entering and leaving, doesn't make noise. While breathing, a person plunges into a state of bright and saturated meditation, but feels its depth only at the end.

During this exercise, inhale and exhale softly to reach the noiselessness of breath; close your eyes for the best concentration. The purpose is to realize the energy of breath: when you practice, you will feel the stream of energy, which is different from a stream of air. Usually people feel how energy flows in a circle from the heart to the forehead and back, but you can have other individual sensations.

For example, I can feel how the energy overflows me and transcends my physical limits.

It is useful to breathe silently for a few seconds, and then gradually increase the amplitude of breathing. As breaths and exhalations become deeper and louder, pay attention to the strength and energy of your breath and continue to increase the amplitude along with the energy. If you increase the amplitude too quickly, you will lose strength and your breathing will turn into work instead of pleasure.

Such a technique gives a person the opportunity to feel their breath, mind, and body. It's especially useful for people with breathing problems and it is often used to treat colds. This method is fascinating; while doing it, the majority of people experience such pleasure that they are eager to breathe this way constantly. This breathing is good for meditation and, as it is well known, meditation not only helps to solve problems, but also opens up new prospects. Spending time meditating after a breathwork session, with added Reiki energy, is a very vigorous and life-giving mix.

VI. "Ten short and one long." Twenty-two connected respiratory cycles, done after repeating a sequence of ten short and one long inhale-exhale, twice. It is important to change the rhythm of your breaths from time to time. When you master the conscious breath, the varied rhythm will become natural.

This practice will help you to manage your breath in a stressful situation. When you are worried, strained, or afraid to speak to someone, the breath fades in the thorax. At that moment, it's necessary to give a command to the brain and to force yourself to start breathing as you do when exercising.

VII. "Free style." Twenty connected respiratory cycles in whichever beat gives you the greatest pleasure. In this exercise, the rhythm remains up to you. If you feel intuition during this exercise, it means that you are capable of feeling a stream of energy through breath and put its rhythm in a harmony and energy.

Besides the obvious advantages and the pleasure of these breathing exercises, you may also feel unpleasant sensations in the body and even physical torture, sensations that are connected with hyperventilation. Hyperventilation is a medical term which means over-breathing. It can cause a variety of symptoms. For example, rapid difficult and irregular breathing, trembling or prickling in the hands or feet, dizziness, faintness, hysterical crying, irrational sense of fear and horror, a faint sensation of discharge from the body or pressure in different parts of the body, strong inflow of energy, instability of body temperature, a partial blackout, claustrophobia, headache, orgasmic sensations, spiritual and religious visions, bright telepathic experiences, nausea, dryness of mouth, ringing or noise in the ears, memories of birth or somnambulistic state, euphoria and pleasurable conditions, bright imaginings and sharp perceptions of color, and death and revival experiences. Most of the symptoms described occur during the liberation of the suppressed psychophysical memories that flash through your mind during holotropic breathing. They quickly disappear during nasal breathing.

These symptoms are the result of old, negative thoughts; breathe through them, and they will all be gone. This is called *breathing the problem out*! The onset of symptoms means that there is progress in the healing process, where the main doctor is the breath itself. You will feel your consciousness departs. At Leonardo Orr's Inspiration Institute, we began each day with respiratory gymnastics which improved our mood remarkably!

So breathe and smile!

COMING TO THE USA

Thursday, March 13, 2008

My acquaintance with this country began with a couple of funny incidents in Moscow. Leonardo Orr's book, with the colorful description of his Inspiration Institute in sunny California, made a very strong impression on me. I decided to go there and feel the charm of breathing in the water by myself—I didn't know about such breathing techniques at that time. Having exchanged a couple of e-mails with the Institute, I received the e-mailed description how to get from Moscow to Charlottesville, with a connected flight in Atlanta. And as I'd never heard about Charlottesville, I was pretty sure that is was located somewhere in California. The whole process took almost half a year, including the invitation and visa application.

It turned out that getting the visa was quiet easy. The officer in a window simply asked, "Are you a university professor?" and I automatically answered yes. "And do you want the visa for . . . ?" Despite several years of studying English, I understood only about 90 percent of American English at that time. Without having understood what he actually told me about the visa and not wishing to ask again, I answered yes. He handed me the payment receipt and there I saw the amount I had already paid in the consular center while handing in the documents. I had been so sure that I had already paid for the visa and that there would be no more additional expenses that I had simply left my money at home that morning. I hadn't even checked if I had any cash in my handbag. When I asked a Russian girl, an employee of the embassy, about the sum, she pointed at the visa duration period and exclaimed, "It's a two-year visa!" Pleasure and pressure mingled in my mind. Pleasure because I finally understood the meaning of the words said to me by the officer and the pressure came from a convulsive thought: do I have any money on me now? The most surprising thing was that I happened to have the exact amount in my bag—neither more nor less.

The next steps were even easier: the ticket, the flight, and I arrived in Charlottesville. At the beginning of March it was only 10-12°C instead of the promised 25°C in California. My first morning was rather cold—only 8°C and the next week it didn't get any warmer. I thought I was in California and I had only T-shirts and shorts to wear. A week later, feeling completely frozen and observing people mostly in gloves and scarves, I asked the manager of the Institute, "Is it California?" She laughed and said that they had sold that center five years ago. After that, I had to put on warmer clothes, even though I didn't bring any from Moscow. I had meant to fly to California!

Another cultural shock I experienced was at the Atlanta airport, where I saw giant people. I had never imagined people of such size before because my assumptions about Americans were based on Hollywood films. I thought they would all be tall, slim, and very beautiful. At the airport, I was surrounded by giants who looked very happy and did not feel uncomfortable. In Russia, such people would always feel uncomfortable. On the second day of my arrival to the US, we went to a local supermarket, an enormous building with a huge parking lot where tank-like Range Rovers were parked. That was the first time I saw them in such quantities. And then I saw people unloading from their vehicles and understood something about America—there would always be an over-abundance of food, things, people! When I entered the supermarket, I realized that I wanted to live there forever. Yes, in a supermarket! Although I had traveled through almost all of Europe and lived in Moscow, where the system of supermarket chains is highly developed, there were so many different jars and boxes that I had never seen before. When I tried to grab one of them, it was snatched from my hands and one of my companions shouted "No! You cannot!" And it was true, I should not. Everything was either artificial or made with additives. Dairy products are artificial as well and that's why everyone has to drink soy milk, which tastes like rubbish. The only way out is so-called "organic food," but somehow natural cucumbers and tomatoes are very rare.

THE FIRST DAY.
THE BEGINNING

Friday, March 14, 2008

    I couldn't wait for the training to start, but I had arrived a day early. To my surprise, I found out that I could start immediately if I wished. In Orr's new center, Inspiration University, the entire staff of rebirthers works under the guidance of Peace. It's her spiritual name, which she took because she needed peace in her soul and calmness in her heart. She was about fifty-five years old, very charming and independent, mainly because she grew up in a Sicilian family of musicians. Since her childhood, she lived with freedom and a lack of organization. She had been Leonardo's student for a long time and the administration of the center was a kind of a trial period for her.

    Another rebirther working at the Inspiration University is Ariel. When I heard her spiritual name for the first time I had an association with the Disney's cartoon, *The Little Mermaid*. She looked like an alien with her beautiful, piercing blue eyes and an absent look on her face. She was twenty-seven years old and had been working with Leonardo, who rescued her from suicide, for two years. The system of professional rebirther training is based on constant practice and experience interchange. So, if a rebirther learns the breathing system and can really feel it during a session, he can then rebirth another one and so on for ten sessions. In Leonardo's opinion, the breathing system should consist of ten sessions because people can't breathe freely until they completely release their breath. After the release, breathing goes freely and automatically. You can usually achieve this effect during the eighth session—breathing becomes effortless.

A month before my arrival at Leonardo's University, Irina, a very spiritually gifted girl, arrived there. She was thirty-four years old and she came from a mixed family—her father was American and her mother was Russian. She had never lived in the United States or in Russia, so she speaks both languages with a very interesting accent. She was tremendously gifted in languages and she could fluently speak five or six. Now she lives in Guatemala and teaches cabbala. She has good healing abilities which she inherited from her mother, who was a born healer. Irina knew only the holotropic breath (a very deep breath with an open throat through the second chakra, to lift the kundalini energy up), so Leonardo's type of breathing came as a surprise to her.

According to Leonardo's technique, breath should go through the nose, with an attention on the fourth chest chakra. I tried to breathe like that, but being used to holotropic breathing for ten years, I felt uncomfortable. So I forced myself to breath in the "right" way and I found that I could not relax. My body began twisting, filled with oxygen and the energy of breath. For me, any act of rebirthing starts with the experience of a birth trauma. My mom was in labor with me for more than a day before doctors gave her a shot of painkillers to stop the pain. The pain was gone; so were the contractions. So, the doctors made a decision to drag me out with forceps. And so I endure all this pain and horror at each session of rebirthing, and nobody could ever help me or explain what was happening. Only the next day it was explained to me that I simply endured the trauma of my birth. So rebirthing for me was always associated with physical pain. Nevertheless, it has a lot of positive benefits. I breathed, my body relaxed, and soon I felt a stream of light and ease in my second chakra. That was enough for the first time.

THE SECOND DAY.
THE BATH

Saturday, March 15, 2008

The bath is a special exercise in Orr's Institute. Frankly speaking, I prefer a shower. But it seemed like there had been too many people thinking like me, and the shower simply did not work. So, bathing became a necessity. The bath was not for relaxation, but for breathing. My psyche couldn't stand it and my body resisted with full force. The point is that breathing in water recreates our prenatal feelings and the sensations that we felt when we were in our mothers' bellies. As I was born with a great difficulty, I had hated water since my childhood. I even hated to wash and did it only under my mom's insistence. In adulthood, water is also related to money. I always could earn as much money as I wanted, but I never wanted to keep anything. I never saved, and I didn't want anything—not a car, nor an apartment.

Yet in that Institute, for the first time, I felt the desire to take a bath and to breathe in it. Lying there, I had the sensation of water as a vital component of life. A life stream—warmth and tenderness—washed over me, as if I were in the maternal womb. The second breath is easy; you want to breathe with the full lungs. I plunged into a light slumber, almost like coma, meditation, I wasn't afraid of closing my eyes, and after some time I felt that the water almost covered my ears . . .

After the bath, I experienced the desire to sit by a fire for the first time. Again, everything felt simple and as plain as the nose on your face. Sensations of absolute harmony and love for myself. The body was relaxed but at the same time was ready to work. I clearly understood that at the conscious level, communication worked with the four elements—fire, earth, water, air—and the life's most important element—love. God bless simplicity!

THE THIRD DAY.
FROM NOW ON I AM PEARL!

Sunday, March 16, 2008

That day, Elvie conducted a session with me. Elvie, a rebirther with twenty years' experience, was very charming, sincere, and light. Even now, describing her, the sensation of ease and tenderness remains. Her sincerity won our hearts when at breakfast, seeing all of us for the first time, she openly shared with us the problems of her divorce and told about the forced parting with her daughter, all without hiding her tears. It was very touching.

Before beginning the session, I realized how much I missed my daughter. I started to breathe and my body began to unscrew and seize again. And here the voice of Elvie, seemingly from nowhere, sounded like a rescue, "It is absolutely unessential to endure a birth trauma each time!" It seemed simple this time. My breath calmed down at once, my body relaxed, and vivifying energy began to fill my free body. I saw a beautiful seashore and saw myself in the body of Aphrodite, being born from sea foam. And I saw a glittering pinkish seashell in my hands. I opened it and found a large live pearl there. I heard a voice in my head that said that I would now have a spiritual name—Pearl. Pearl means cleanliness, and as spirituality for me means cleanliness first of all, that moment I understood that I had reached it. Even though I had been a spiritual teacher since 2005, I had doubted myself and considered myself unworthy of my mission because of insufficient cleanliness. Spirituality is not theory, but a life and incessant work. For me this pearl became an original award and recognition of my work.

THE FOURTH DAY.
DAY OF FIRE AND FAST

Monday, March 17, 2008

Today was a fasting day. Up until that time I knew only one meaning of the word fast—something quick, swift, or rapid. Because of this, when it was announced to us that the next day would be a fasting day, I didn't react in any way. I had a feeling that it was somehow connected with meals but I didn't understand exactly how, and I decided to wait until the next day to find out. In the morning, after my bath, which lasted thirty minutes instead of the usual hour prescribed, I went to the kitchen and took a pear from a vase with fruits. The startled voice of a Canadian participant stopped me, "It is impossible!" I was surprised, and she once again solemnly declared that today was a fasting day, which still didn't mean anything to me. Then I found out that the word fast means to be without food for some time and the word breakfast, accordingly, means to interrupt an absence of food. Now words make more sense to me and I'm pretty interested in the original meaning of the Russian word for breakfast. My thoughts brought me back to my stomach, which was persistently demanding some food.

It was rather cold, approximately 10 °C. We were told that we would go to the woods, to sit by a fire. *Well that's fine*, I thought. *I will sit, get some warmth, read a book.* I didn't want to participate and gather wood. I don't like physical work. We got in cars and set off—everything was nice and cozy. This coziness ended when we were taken out to a forest and told that everyone would need to start his own fire and to keep it up until the sun goes down (from 10 a.m. to 6 p.m.). I felt such rage, something I hadn't felt for a long time. Freezing cold, empty stomach, and with just a liter of water, we had to collect firewood. Moreover, the wood needed to be cut with a saw which I'd never used before. I kindled a fire pretty quickly, but then it constantly needed to be tended, and after four hours of trying I just fell asleep nearby, still angry and rather exhausted. I woke up fresh, vigorous, all-forgiving and ready to say goodbye to the fire. While I was trying to keep the fire up, I realized once again that physical activity is not interesting for me and that I prefer intellectual activity. Overall, the primitive life is not for me. It may offer us some historical insight, but I believe that everyone is born in his own time. Since I live in the twenty-first century things, the technologies of this time interest me the most. I should understand, accept, learn to use and develop them further; otherwise there will be nothing to leave our descendants. I respect the habits of those who think otherwise. But more often people don't accept novelty because of other reasons—fear or laziness. Personally, I need some time to adjust myself to new electronic inventions and I usually grumble, *What does it do for me?, I was perfectly happy without these features.* Yes, it is not for me, and not for those who don't accept it; it is for new generations who, having no doubts, will use these features, whatever they may be.

And here again comes a question about the struggle between old and new. But there isn't any struggle, actually! New things will always be more progressive and more attractive than old things because they offer more comfortable decisions. And then a person just has to make a choice. There is nothing inherently good or bad in either option. For in God, everything is equal. Therefore it is possible to understand why He doesn't stop immediately those processes which are, let's put it this way, uncomfortable for people—fascism or terrorism, for example. These are all toys, from His point of view.

Sitting there on the bank of some American brook and looking at my dying fire, I understood that I had a choice. I got up and went on collecting branches. And once again I had some thoughts about the balance of materiality and spirituality. Where is the line and who is to draw it?

Another student at the Institute, Chris, worked as a hospital attendant or a nurse in a morgue. He said that his aim was to help people die. He was married, had a two-year-old daughter, and he believed that the world is better to be observed from outside; God gives all that you ask for.

And then I thought, why should I ask God for trivial things if I'm perfectly capable of getting them by myself? He created me in His image and likeness and that means I can do things for myself! Although I understand that for God everything that He gives is the same, whether it's a crust of bread or a Mercedes, I wish to get what I want by myself and to feel a little bit like God. And I don't think that it will somehow belittle the advantages God brings. And I don't think it belittles His or my virtue.

I was running with a writing book and a ball-point pen around the fire, throwing some twigs into it as I had to keep it up for at least three more hours. And then I realized one simple thing. It is possible to do everything with both hands: one is to support something physically, the second is to support something spiritually. Life as meditation, but without fanaticism, without leaving for an astral, without receiving magnificent images and idleness on arrival. On the contrary: I came, I saw, I made it. So I continued collecting branches!

I brought enough branches and the fire burned so-so on one side. And here the wind blew suddenly—the fire shot up, revived. And here I felt a hand and the presence of God in everything . . . even in this fire, which flashed unexpectedly, in the wood filled with the sunshine, in branches which were everywhere—they only needed to be seen. And quite unexpectedly, I was able to see all this profusion and God in it. He was talking to me through the whisper of leaves, last year's leaves, the fire crackling and a water pearl. I understood that I heard God. These are not big words. Having felt the world in all its depth, I realized that people are looking for God anywhere, but not in themselves. They want to perceive Him only as a miracle, a New Year's gift, but not as a daily reality. What for? Is there anything interesting in this mundane reality? The reality is an everyday life, and for the majority of people, it is boring and routine. But if you take a look at this boredom and routine through the eyes of others (I have understood now what it means to be enlightened), which now means to me to be inside the light or to be touched by the light, it will be outstanding! I always hear questions like, so now what, do we all have to go to America to get some enlightenment? The point is not the place itself, but instead the desire to get to know yourself, your image and . . .

After some time, I grew to like collecting branches and God was helping me to keep the fire up. Here came the understanding that it is necessary to be ready for enlightenment. Not everyone really needs it and not everyone is really prepared. And one more realization: after all the suffering and torture we undergo, everything will be all right. I remembered the beginning of that day: full of rage and physical weariness, and there I was at the end of the day—talking to

God. I was smiling like a lunatic, I could feel and I see His light and presence; I felt a bit shy, like there was someone standing next to me. I experienced sensations of reality and impossibility at the same time. Miracles! I had never thought that enlightenment was possible for an average person. I always considered it to be a privilege reserved for the chosen ones.

One more thought came to me when I went to get some more branches: you need to be ready for anything. That morning in the kitchen I heard a man muttering "yummy" to his child, while persuading him to eat. If I hadn't learned this English word three months before my arrival to the center, I wouldn't have reacted to it at all. So a picture of the relationship between the parent and the child was painted clearly for me. All other processes have the same scheme. If we are already in a process, it extends for us, goes deeper; if we aren't, then we are running along a coastline and swearing that we aren't floating. And somehow we don't think about swimming by ourselves or asking a trainer to help us; it seems to be too much work. All we think about is a champion cup for our breaststroke.

Why breaststroke, instead of freestyle?

I just liked the word. In one old Russian movie, *Morozka*, there was a phrase: "Are you warm enough, sweetie?" when we were kids, we all watched this film and then watched it with our kids, laughing at the unreal Marphushenka's requirements. Somehow we don't want to see ourselves this way. But we act just like that because of the incompatibility of our requirements and reality. And this, I would say, is the biggest problem of the mankind—the desire to get everything without making any effort. The problem is that it's possible only in fairytales. And those who tried to make fairytales out of their lives failed. So did I, when I decided not to collect branches and just stare at the others.

"And what if I don't want to be enlightened? Do we have to work? Can we just get an 'advance payment'?" Sure you can, but your efforts should come first, please.

We all have different wishes and only God knows what qualities we need to make them happen. We all are the creators of our desires, not our parents or Santa Claus. God teaches us to be just like Him, to work miracles on our own. To develop these qualities we face the situations in which we can show our worth, believe in our miracles, and eventually discover a wizard in ourselves!

THE FIFTH DAY.
REBIRTHING WITH MICHAEL

Tuesday, March 18, 2008

Michael, a rebirther from Australia, was an American in his late forties. He had never had a family, and therefore he was used to doing everything independently and was not used to sharing. He had no desire to care about somebody—he was by himself. As a geologist, he traveled to Australia a few years ago for a job. There, he learned rebirthing with Sandra Ray (a well-known student of Leonardo Orr) and returned to America with the desire to start a new life. He had never tried other exercises for energy flow, only rebirthing. Therefore, when communicating with him, I didn't feel the salutary aura that usually comes from a person who professionally works with energy. It was interesting to me, how could he help me even though he didn't know any energy practices. Getting ahead, I will say that for a rebirther, it is very important to be a healer as well because during sessions there are so many situations when it is necessary to help the client and simple supervision and physical presence is not enough. I had always considered this my personal opinion, but after talking with people from different countries and different continents (Canada, Guatemala, Australia, the United States), my opinion was confirmed.

During rebirthing, the person can feel different sensations—from powerful energy lifting to difficulty breathing. In both cases energy support works wonders: in the first case, it lifts a person to a new level; in the second, it helps to un-stick a person.

I was curious about how Michael was going to carry out the session. He asked me three questions, which I had to answer with the help of breath. My greatest problem appeared to be my doubts about my ability to be a spiritual teacher, owing to my age and experience. In my imagination I had pictures of fathers in churches, respected Indian gurus of an infinite age. Moreover, I didn't fit because I had a family of my own and I wasn't a person brought up in a monastery or in a religious and devotional family. In general, I had many conflicting thoughts. I sat and started breathing; my body twisted again, my hands and feet were filled with weight and I didn't know what to do with myself.

That moment Michael surprised me the most, saying that I should stop moving and start to breathe toward the place where it was the most unpleasant! I understood then that it was my head; I could feel all its parts—my temples, forehead, eyes, ears. They all were compressed, as though somebody was squeezing them with an iron hoop.

And it was as though an iron elevator were pressed down so that my head was right on my shoulders. I understood that this symbolized the environment I lived in—bosses, people, parents, all my obligations and promises I had made of my own free will.

To breathe against this elevator was very difficult. Breath was confused and interrupted all the time and the lift was pressing down on me even more. The body tried to resist, dashing, twitching, turning, jumping up and Michael was constantly trying to stop these attempts, insisting on breathing and "breathing out" these physiological conditions (breathe a problem out means to realize, accept and integrate it).

After approximately thirty minutes of this torture, the fingers on my right hand started doing some strange movements and composing different figures which were quite similar to mudras. My left palm rose in a vertical position and there was a bright, white light in front of my eyes. I had seen a similar light some years ago and I understood that it was the Lord. I was curious about who was being sent to me now. And then my right hand started to cross myself if in church and I understood that it was Jesus Christ. After some time the light gathered in the middle of my left palm and I understood that I was being given an opportunity of initiation on this spiritual conductor. The light amplified again, my right palm composed a mudra and there was God Shiva, and the light filled my left palm. Then my palms started to make movements like making ablution but without any water, I bent and sang, *Amen*, understanding that Mohammed had come. The most interesting thing of all this was that I actually didn't belong to any religious faith and I didn't feel comfortable in our orthodox churches with its crowds of people and strange rituals. But during this rebirthing, I observed myself from the outside and felt that some internal force was pushing me and I was performing these rituals internally, like my body knew more than my mind. All these movements were filled with deep inner meaning for me. And if I had already met Buddha in the meditations and I was sure that I wasn't mad, rituals of prayers to Jesus, and especially to Mohammed, were improbable in terms of the sensations I was getting inside my mind and my body. I really felt the vibrations of these spiritual conductors. I had a clear understanding—Christ, Mohammed and Buddha they are just conductors and each of us can be a conductor of that feeling or talent we believe in. For me, the conductor is a person who sincerely loves what he or she does, and is devoted to it—my own approach to life and work.

Ideally, everybody should want to perform ritual actions effortlessly—with a sincere desire, not out of habit. Frankly, I can tell that I still don't have any reaction to rituals. But now I have a body sensation of the Lord presence on each geographical territory. I began to see very accurately the thought-form protecting every country and dominating over it. For example, why did all these deities come to me in America? Because America accepts and allows people of any faith. In Russia no other religion except Christianity can dominate. We Russians are under Jesus Christ's and the Mother of God's protection. Patrons of other religious faiths protect only those who exist within the limits of their religion. It is very restricted and personal. That's why it was not necessary for us to support orthodoxy throughout all the years of Soviet rule. More likely, it had been protecting us and has revived again by itself.

THE SIXTH DAY.
REBIRTHING WITH IRINA

Wednesday, March 19, 2008

I decided that during to work with Irina on my fear of darkness and heights. I realized my fear of darkness the previous night and I felt determination to deal with it. And the second fear, heights, I took to keep the first one company. Where there is the one, there is also the second. Logically I couldn't think of any reasons for these fears, which meant that they came from somewhere deep in my subconscious.

I started to breathe and saw an entrance to the nine-storey block of flats in which I lived at that time, and I was afraid to take a step. And then all my fears rolled onto me: I was afraid to be alone, I was afraid to be lost in an unfamiliar place, I was afraid to leave the house and to forget to lock the door, I was afraid to lose my mobile phone and all numbers in it. And suddenly I saw my maternal grandmother. She always seemed an angel to me, someone who had descended from heaven to join us on earth. There was something—inhuman about her universal kindness, her love, her pure, sky-blue eyes. I have never seen such blue eyes in again. My grandmother and my grandfather lived in Ukraine, and he often abused her. The strangest thing was that the grandmother always took it in stride. When I saw her during my meditation, I asked why she didn't resist.

She answered that she was an angel, and angels don't feel the same way people feel. They are more than a physical body. Then I saw a bright, dark blue light where my third eye should be and heard her words, "You can read people's thoughts." Suddenly it became clear where I had inherited all these thoughts about angels, and I started asking her what kind of angel I am. A deep green bright light, which symbolizes the angel Raphael, came. It enclosed a green lime in my right palm and told me that I would be able to cure people. The sensations were amazing! The palm and fingers of my right hand were moving by themselves as though they were healing. But I write this now, months after I first discovered this gift. Now I dare to feel myself a healer and am no longer constrained by my fears.

Later, when we were sharing our sensations, Leonardo noted that there are four levels of healing; the highest level is to be a conductor of infinite spirit. It was that very sensation of a conductor which I had received. I can cure at the spiritual level and, if it is necessary, I can use all the other levels of healing. But I understood it only after the returning from the USA, in the course of practice. I treat every client differently, so I healed one client with the help of candles (though I've never read anything about it); another, I fumigated with herbs, just observing my hands from outside. But the spiritual healing is faster and more effective because I can see the real cause of an illness or problem. I start the healing process by asking a question, without knowing exactly how I'm going to heal someone. The process is very simple: I refocus the client's attention from consequences (illness) to the cause (an event or experience the psyche hasn't coped with that is troubling the physical body). That's why the body is ill; this traumatic event or experience is repressed by the person who is trying to forget it. It's really pretty simple!

THE SEVENTH DAY.
OM SHANTY!

Thursday, March 20, 2008

The morning began, as always, with an hour of breathing in a bath. Then we, joyful and fresh, gathered downstairs, joined hands, sat down in a circle, and started letting out sounds. These sounds were the sounds of love, pleasure, and greeting. This practice serves as a happiness and charge mantra for the whole day. Some more traditional morning activities were respiratory gymnastics: twenty connected respiratory cycles through the nose; then another twenty cycles, but with inhalation through the nose and exhalation through the mouth; and another twenty cycles of silent breathing through the nose. Then we had a reading of positive affirmations and an exchange of impressions. The night before, I'd had a thought that in general some people want to play with big money, and some people are just lazy.

After a morning bath, I felt an irresistible desire to realize the idea that had appeared to me during the evening seminar "Financial Prosperity"—to enter the international market, though I didn't know how I could begin, since I was in some small American town that wasn't even on most maps! I went outdoors—I decided to knock someone's door and offer my services right there, knowing nothing about those people and their interests. I was completely horrified and began to search for some reason not to do it. At last I collected my thoughts, approached a house, and found out that there was no button to press because there was no bell on the door! *Yeah*! I thought, *I don't need to do it*! But then I realized that I still had to do it. I knocked on the door of the next house, but nobody answered, and I just went down the road, having decided that I would meet somebody somehow.

The problem is that in America, especially in small towns, nobody goes anywhere on foot. There are no sidewalks, there are only good asphalt roads and everybody drives cars similar to tanks or tractors. The city in American life means movement and people walking on streets. In the town where the center was located, I saw people only in the supermarkets, entering or leaving church, and getting into their cars. To go to a small town without having your own transportation is impossible in America. It seems like people there are born in cars.

But a moment later, I saw a girl who was taking garbage to the dustbin. Having filled my lungs with air, I shouted to her, "Excuse me!" I surprised myself with my force and persistence. But when I approached her, all my confidence disappeared. I was terrified; the tears began to run down my cheeks, but there was no way to give up. And I began by saying "I live next to you and I am engaged in a course called 'Money and Prosperity.' I would like to ask which of my services could interest you right now? I am Russian, I can speak two languages, I can offer Reiki sessions, angel card–readings, and I have a camera and can take a picture of you." The last one came to mind just from feebleness. Impatiently, I was expecting a reply to the effect of, "Thanks, but I don't need anything right now!" and that's what I got. My God, how happy I was to hear it and to leave that place as soon as possible. On my way back, I understood that for the first time in my life I had taken the negative answer positively, with pleasure and unconscious relief. A victory! It was the victory over white and black, good and bad, positive and negative. There is no division; there is only acceptance, harmony, pleasure, and happiness. "Om Shanty!" (in Sanskrit that means, "a peaceful soul!")

After that seminar, I understood that my negative feelings about working for "the big money" were connected to the fact that even a small sum provoked a huge stream of energy, which was literally burning me inside out. Each time when I had to pay a bill, a huge stream of energy rose through my body to my head—my cheeks flared and temples pulsed. Therefore I tried not to think about the big money; I didn't dare to even think of exact figures, or an amount I was hoping to earn. The work continued.

THE EIGHTH DAY.
I AM A REBIRTHER FOR CHRIS

Friday, March 21, 2008

That morning I became a rebirther myself. Remembering recommendations from Leonardo Orr—that it is important to concentrate on breath instead of shouting, as I had during my first ten sessions. Then it would be possible to use any technique: it would be possible to shout, but breathing would be better. It is necessary to point out that I planned to conduct the session in English, which demanded double concentration. My client, Chris, was a very spiritually developed person. I know that he was twenty-eight years old, married, had a two-year-old daughter, and literally lived in harmony with nature, in the forest. The offer to become his rebirther came unexpectedly, but I knew that sometimes it's better not to think and just say yes and sort things out later, so I agreed. I should mention that I had already refused previously, during the second day of my stay at the center. I was coming down from the second floor, shining and joyful after a breathing session. My feeling of enlightenment radiated from me. And then I saw a man sitting right on a dirty floor who looked like a tramp. There was no chance of just slipping away, no way to disappear and hide my openness and glow. When I greeted him, he lifted his eyes, like Buddha's, and began to speak to me about my enlightenment, which he had instantly noticed. I was puzzled and became locked—I retired deeply into myself. For me, it was a good lesson about the discrepancy between external and internal. I do agree with A.P.Chekhov, our Russian writer, that "everything should be beautiful in the person: both mind and appearance."[1] Then I became great friends with Chris because his spiritual depth amazed me. My mission was to turn him back toward reality and tune him into the human program on the Earth. Two weeks later, when we were saying good-bye with tears running down our cheeks, he whispered to me, "Let's meet again when I have opened a rebirthing center of my own and have made my first fifty thousand dollars!" It was the victory of a reality over insufficiency!

When I began the session with Chris, I decided that it was necessary to relax and trust my intuition. Chris asked how I usually carried out sessions because he had just started to study rebirthing. After his first breath work session in this Center, he even wanted to leave, but stayed and believed in the force of rebirthing and eventually felt it. When he started to breathe, my right hand suddenly began to move and radiate green light and my left hand started radiating white light—the healing process began. After the session Chris told me that he physically felt how the block was leaving him, how his body was relaxing and how relief was filling him entirely. As he said, it was magic. And he asked for one more rebirthing session. During the session I felt like an open and pure channel of energy and for the first time I cured with my eyes open, though usually it was more comfortable for me to heal with closed eyes.

---

[1]   A.P.Chekhov "Unkle Ivan", Pravda, Moscow, 1985

In the evening Leonardo explained that there are four levels of participation of a rebirther in the course of a session with a client:

1. the simple presence of a rebirther during a session is a means of supervising the client's breath and movement of the thorax
2. kundalini breathing: when the client starts to breathe deeply and strongly and his or her breath incorporates kundalini energy,
3. the rebirther can feel this movement of energy; the rebirther sees the energy and its movement, observes all visions and the conditions occurring to the client
4. the rebirther becomes the channel of divine energy, which helps the client without actively participating

All levels can occur during one session. Therefore, it is not enough for a rebirther to have only *some* technical knowledge. It is necessary to possess intuition, the third eye, vision, and thought-reading—and to be a healer first of all. Breathing basically cures by itself, therefore it is possible to breathe on your own, which is something I always recommend, but only after a course of training (group or individual). Without the proper assistance, a person can't go very deep—the fear of not returning is overwhelming. Therefore only superficial problems are solved. For deeper, older problems, it is better to breathe with an experienced healer-rebirther.

During a session, the body can experience different states—from physical pain to psychological panic. To remove such symptoms it is necessary to breathe right through them. The pain comes from the negative experiences we have had encountered with in our lives, but emotionally we don't want to leave that pain behind as it is valuable for us as part of our memory. This experience makes us living people.

Having gotten rid of pain and mental sufferings, we live on a new spiritual level and we get nearer to God. He didn't suffer and also didn't want us to! He, at the moment of crucifixion, was already not in His body, but in the soul outside of the physical body. When a rebirther gets to the highest level, he or she ceases to feel pain and physical sensations at all. That had just happened with me. For the first time, I didn't feel any physical symptoms in my body, but at the same time I saw that the process of my healing was very strong because when I was removing the blockage, my breathing evened and my body relaxed. Om Shanty!

THE NINTH DAY.
MY REBIRTHING WITH CHRIS

Saturday, March 22, 2008

This time, Chris was my rebirther. He used meditation to immerse me in my sensations, but nevertheless I was breathing. I remember that sometimes I ceased to breathe and plunged into myself, but his voice each time returned me to breathing. I received the pearl and heard the voice again. That time, I thought that someday I would be able to cure with the help of my voice, but it would take some time to work on. And just as I predicted, about six months later, after I had once again gone to America and attended a seminar "Healing Sounds Intensive" by a well-known composer Jonathan Goldman, I began to cure with sound and voice. The speed of materialization of what the person sees in meditation depends only on his or her readiness to accept it. Right at the end of the rebirthing session, again I saw a white light escaping from a dark abyss, which meant immortality. I was frightened again, but it wasn't as interesting for me that time. But as it was happening the second time, I persuaded myself to enter into this light. The sensations were strong! The light captured my entire body; it stretched, twisted like a candy wrapper, and filled me with vital energy—it was like receiving the gift of youth! It was the very thing I needed! Subsequently, at Goldman's seminar, I received the ability to change people's DNA. And once again, this ability proved the correctness of my internal sensation.

Not to be so afraid, it is advisable for inexperienced rebirthers not to conduct an independent meditation and rebirthing on death. Close your eyes and answer the first questions about death that come to your mind—How old will you be when you die? Where, why, or what will you die from?—and then start to breathe there. I also liked Leonardo's thought that immortality doesn't guarantee cleanliness. The person can be immortal, but can still be silly, etc. For example, the devil is immortal.

THE TENTH DAY.
MY REBIRTHING WITH ARIEL

Sunday, March 23, 2008

That day Ariel, the beautiful girl with blue eyes from Michigan, worked with me. Some years ago she had nearly died after opening herself to the ability to see the energy of other people. She was rescued by somebody's words that she was an "indigo child" needed to learn and professionally develop her abilities.

In the morning I felt that I should work with "a tummy of the guru," as excess weight in the area of the third chakra (solar plexus). That is where our first or second brain lives, and it does what it wants. People who have excess weight there usually have salutary abilities. This chakra takes up everything we face in the world: all the pain, worries, and problems of other people, and, if we just accept such feelings, we can heal them, cures. Therefore all diets and physical exercise in this case become useless. It is necessary to clear the third chakra—to sit by a fire, to breathe in a warm bath, and to fast once a week. But I had been doing all these things already, except for the fire purification, because I had an apartment instead of the house. Anyway, I wanted to find my own quick and effective way of purification.

And one more question worried me. I always liked to open different abilities in people that they had never suspected, and thereby lift them to a higher intellectual or intuitive level. It seemed like no problem for me! Yes, when I carry out my frequent sessions, the intuition works ideally and I attract those who need me at this point. But when I work at the university, I receive ready-made groups, not groups that I would have assembled myself. Even then, I try to choose the best of the best but my level of knowledge is still considerably higher than what they want and are ready to receive. I thought that it was only my problem. But when I started to think about this discrepancy, I came across the film *Mona Lisa Smile,* with Julia Roberts. I decided to watch it, mostly because of the actresses, not the plot. The story takes place in 1953-1954 in America, in a Wellesley College, a private, all-girls liberal arts college from wealthy families. Roberts plays the art professor who, tired of the primitiveness of her former pupils, arrived at Wellesley with hope of teaching highly intellectual young women. Instead she met living dolls—girls who were well-groomed, textbook smart, and spiritually underdeveloped. The professor experiences a crisis because her expectations are not met. Certainly, she sees changes in her students, but it's not enough; they are still not doing what they're capable of. I feel just the same when I taught marketing classes to MBA students (Master of Business Administration). Many years ago I also decided to take a chance and began to teach a course at the university, "Marketing in English." It was interesting and difficult for me at the same time. At that point, I had expected students from the "cream of the Russian business society." But gradually my interests had changed, and I didn't feel the necessity to explain the obvious any more. People were receiving results at their level and I wanted them to rise to mine.

Bearing all those ideas in mind, I started to breathe. Instantly all the muscles of my head braided. And the pain was so strong that it seemed like my head was going to explode. It was difficult to breathe; that's why my breath was constantly interrupted. My entire body was clenched: I could feel that my hands were twisted and my feet were filled with lead. I wasn't able to breathe under this physical condition and my rebirther was constantly focusing my attention on the solar plexus. After some time, I disconnected and plunged into the depths of unconsciousness. As the matter of fact, I don't remember what was happened there. Once I regained consciousness, I saw the yellow angel illuminating my body and saw myself as a little child swaying on a crescent in a shape of a swing. Also I heard a voice that told me I was a child of the moon. Then I physically felt as if my physical body rose vertically and was swaying on a swing. It was fantastic—lightness, freedom, satisfaction!

After the session Ariel told me that she saw many lights and much energy coming from my body, especially when I departed to the unconscious. My skin was shining, energy rushed under my skin, and each part of my body relaxed and radiated light. And also she felt that I was loved very much by my parents and they looked after me very well.

The same day, I was the witness of Eric's session, the young twenty-seven-year-old man who was teaching yoga. He had been playing with breath for a long time, but had never tried rebirthing. He had already had four sessions; today was his fifth. He was constantly departing from his unconscious and didn't want to observe the processes running inside him. I saw how Ariel was carrying out the session: she was constantly breathing along with him and encouraging him, telling him, "You can do more for your body."

And it proved once again for me: everywhere energy is necessary, the rebirther's presence is not enough. The rebirther should also possess energy techniques to start the process and to finish it.

During a breathing session, when a person sinks into a sleep, it is possible to ask him or her to do the following exercise: raise the outstretched arms to shoulder level when inhaling and lower them when exhaling. It is also possible to ask a person to kneel or even to stand and to return constantly to twenty connected respiratory cycles. There is one more strategy for working with someone, if the person gives up breathing: allow the person to sleep, as long as possible (from ten minutes up to four hours), while the rebirther does something else, like taking a shower, or going for a walk. Then, the rebirther returns and begins the session as though nothing has happened. It is also useful for the client to walk on hands or knees, which also clears up energy.

During our exchange of impressions, Leonardo told me that the unwillingness to breathe and drift instead into a meditative dream are connected with the usage of strong addictives (drugs, alcohol) in the past. It is possible, but I don't know for sure.

THE ELEVENTH DAY.
MY REBIRTHING WITH LEONARDO ORR

Monday, March 24, 2008

It was very interesting for me to know what "rebirthing: $1,000 for a session" meant. We went to a room and I understood that it was cold and uncomfortable and that I was angry because I had been awakened the previous night by the sound of children crying and other noises downstairs. Then I couldn't fall asleep for a pretty long time owing to the seven hours' difference between Moscow and Atlanta; in Moscow it was the morning already and my body in Atlanta refused to fall asleep at night. The next day I had a headache and desperately wanted to return home to my family. Leonardo began to ask me what I wanted from the session and then my tears started to flow and all my feebleness emerged. Having cried as much as I needed to, I started to breathe. Just to breathe, understanding that nothing was happening and that there would be no miracle. There is the breath, but it isn't perceived as a miracle—it's just breath itself. Gradually, I realized that for the first time I was breathing without difficulties: my breath didn't interrupt, I was constantly in consciousness, I did not depart anywhere, I didn't see any pictures, nothing happened, there was only the breath. After some time, I heard that Leonardo had fallen asleep nearby and I began to copy his breath and there was a revolution! It is difficult to describe how my lungs were broadening and filling with air. It felt like a new kind of breathing. But the most tremendous thing happened later: my body was cut in two and the immortal spirit of immortal Babadzhi, in the form of light, entered me and told me that I could cure the fear of death in myself and others. One after another, each deity endowed me with various salutary abilities. Then I felt as if I was covered with a column of light that energetically pressed my body into the floor so that I couldn't move and breathe. I was breathing prana. Although I heard everything that was happening around me, the sensation of the powerful pressure of energy was amazing. For the first time in my life I felt the fifth element, just like the film. After the session it took me three hours to "get down to the ground" and even then, it was difficult for me to walk. Human possibilities are boundless!

THE TWELFTH DAY.
REBIRTHING WITH IRINA

Tuesday, March 25, 2008

In the morning when I was breathing in the bathroom, the breath became gradually easier and more pleasant. I was constantly departing to the light, relaxing and feeling completeness of process. After a bath, it was always desirable to go out into the street to breathe fresh air. I went out and understood that I didn't want to wander without purpose and my legs started going to the shop nearby. I wondered what I needed there. I found myself in the men's department and there I understood how much I missed my family. My family means so much to me; I love them all very much. So I started to grab different items to bring back home as presents; I felt a great pleasure from the process. When I returned to the center we started the exchange of impressions and a "communication check." And there I couldn't stop talking. I didn't even realize how I got talking; I had planned to talk about some other things. But I couldn't help it. I was listening to what I was saying, it was something about how here, in America, I felt like I was visiting a zoo with exotic animals. I had never seen a live hippie or alternative settlements, but here it was popular—people were protesting the system this way. And the system was actually very simple—people live in a system where everything is handed to them. You don't have to think any more and there are no problems. And without problems, as it is known, there is no development and no movement. When during our rebirthing session Irina asked me about what I wanted to work on, I understood that I had no idea, and I decided to leave it as it was. I told her that I missed my family and that morning I had done some shopping for them. She started asking me questions. And there again I realized that I didn't want to be alone because I didn't want to take responsibility for the planning of my free time. It is easier for me to work and pay a travel agency to plan my trips, or to grumble at my husband's lack of creativity. The realization that I am responsible for entertaining myself drained my energy. It was connected with my childhood, as my mum was always forcing me to go to music school, trying to persuade me to participate in certain sports, etc. Basically, I didn't have a choice in how I spent my time. Although when I was choosing by myself, I succeeded in everything. For example, all eight years that I had spent in music school seemed a nightmare for me. But, having received a diploma after my graduation (just one B, all the rest were As), I went back in the fall to take guitar lessons. In two weeks I could play and pick up tunes by myself! Throughout my eight years of music school, I hadn't been able to learn how to play the piano; they said that I had been tone-deaf. In three weeks I had finished a program that should have taken three months! I was waking up at 7 a.m. and played the guitar before going to school, and without any excuses or distractions (visiting the toilet or the kitchen). And after school, starting from 3 p.m., I couldn't put the instrument down. Tennis became my own second choice. My whole life I had dreamed of playing tennis! And, having finished my music school, I started looking for a tennis school . . .

While I was writing the previous sentence I understood what my problem was and I breathed it out later: a fear of making the wrong choice. My first husband was the trainer in that tennis school. And now, from the esoteric point of view (esoteric for me means my internal, intuitive understanding and feelings) I understand that I'm the one who attracted him and a magical love developed, but never fully developed. I grew frightened of the negativity of the resulting marriage and allowed myself to live in near seclusion for seventeen years. As I wrote that sentence, I can no longer believe I was so frightened. We were dating when he first offered and then even insisted on dating. I understand that, probably, it was the way he wanted to control my life. As for me, I wasn't interested in anything beside tennis. So, I was fifteen years old, but I didn't feel myself to be an adult or a well-developed person. I was a child who had grown up with fairytales in her head. I had read fairytales from almost every nation of the world.

Now I can remember only one episode by which I can judge that my actions were interpreted differently than I intended them. I was standing at a wall and hitting the ball, practicing my serve. Pretty tiresome, but a person who has studied in music school knows what patience means. My patience was "iron;" routine never frightened me. But the routine turns to uncertainty if you aren't sure that you're doing everything right. Because you may learn something wrong—again, this comes from my experience in music school. That's why my searching gaze meant that I needed his help, not that I was interested in him as a man. But he thought that I was encouraging him. We became friends, but I didn't think it was anything more and wasn't interested in a man who was seven years older than me.

In our session, I began to breathe and I saw myself in his apartment again. We were talking, and I understood that I wouldn't be able to get out of there. Later, Irina told me that I was breathing for forty minutes and then stopped for thirty minutes and wasn't moving energetically. During that moment I simply fell down into darkness and didn't see anything. Then something happened in my consciousness, and I decided to breathe and this rescued me. I saw myself at the bottom of a deep hole and began to clamber upward. The earth under me was getting flatter with my every step, and soon I got to the surface. I realized that I needed to make a decision at first and then the Universe did all the work for me. This was how I felt from the moment of the divorce. I ceased to appreciate myself because, for me, too many things didn't fit—I couldn't explain to myself those actions which, from my point of view, looked absolutely brutal. I had seen psychological abuse in films and had read about it in books. I felt like a test animal for my first husband. When I went through the labor of pregnancy, I was told that my husband wasn't going to pick me up from the maternity hospital. My consciousness couldn't logically understand it. And then, after two weeks of living with his family, they decided to boycott me. I endured this for three months. Nobody talked to me, nobody approached our baby. And I lived in this nightmare and, like a blind person, didn't see the reality. And when in eight months I became pregnant again, I was so afraid of unpredictability in our relationships and afraid of giving birth once again that I miscarried. I told them that I needed to get to the hospital, but nobody believed me; they were just laughing at me as I walked to the car. I was fainting from loss of blood. My husband came to see me at the hospital several times; he swore that he loved me.

I thought I had lost my mind when, after all this, my father called me one evening and told me that my husband didn't want me to come back home. The next day my father picked me up from the hospital and we went to take away the baby. My husband opened the door as much as the iron chain let him and talked through it. He didn't try to explain anything, and when I asked about the baby he threatened me, "If you try to enter, I will let the dog loose!" They had a huge Newfoundland. We were shocked, but there was nothing to do, so we left. The only thing that saved me from suicide was that I had fallen asleep until my parents returned from work. When I woke up, it was as if I had become another person. I just stopped feeling anything at all; it was as though all my feelings had been taken away from me. I did everything automatically and only because it needed to be done. After three days my father-in-law brought the baby to me. And that time I thought that they all would be given their due for their actions. And I felt this sensation during the rebirthing session— everything came back to them. I saw that they were sorry and gave me everything they should have. When I describe it, I realize that I don't care what they are going through. I can feel myself now; I feel stable and confident again! After this session, my eyes were lit with female force and confidence—so much so that even people around me noticed it. And I felt that the seventeen-year-old girl who had frozen all her emotions had finally grown up!

During this rebirthing session, I entered the space of my ex-husband and felt very bad. All became clear at once: he morally wasn't ready to become a father and even the physical appearance of the baby didn't help to change his behavior and attitude. When our daughter cried, he went to his parents' room and watched cartoons. He didn't understand that the baby was not a toy and at some point his consciousness just gave up. Having realized it during that rebirthing session, I decided that my daughter didn't need that sort of father, and I thanked God that everything happened as it happened. And the reason it took me sixteen years to overcome it became clear to me during the next rebirthing session.

A card of Tarot, which we picked up to designate the process I was in at the time, symbolized water, i.e. fantasies and emotions. Everything depends on our imagination, but things aren't always as they seem to be. Although water always erases borders between reality and myth, it never stops and eliminates obstacles very easily.

THE THIRTEENTH DAY.
A SEMINAR WITH LEONARDO ORR

Wednesday, March 26, 2008

That day Leonardo told us about an interesting kind of breath: breathing through the stomach and lungs simultaneously. No special technique for this breathing is required—you just needed to experience eight sessions of rebirthing. During the eighth session, a person suddenly finds the rhythm and depth of breath that he or she then uses in everyday life. People can't breathe unless they release their breath completely. The free breath is characterized by not forcing yourself to breath—it just happens by itself. You can get to this point at the eighth session of rebirthing. When a person can't breathe or has a nose running or a sore throat—it is necessary for him to breathe. When people are born and can't breathe, doctors spank them to help them to make the first breath.

Leonardo could breathe freely only twenty eight years after he had started to practice breathing techniques, in 2002. When we breathe coherently, we connect a practice of breath with kundalini energy and in thirty seconds we get to a transcendental condition where we can remain as long as we want. I began to use this technique of breathing during a new training, the "Art of harmonious relationships," which was aimed at the comprehension of your role, the role of your children, and the roles within a family (husband, wife, and child), as well as pregnancy and other things that accompany familial happiness.

Relaxation is another way to live a long, happy life, but stress kills. We are not simply bodies, but spirits. We don't need to come back to God—we are already with Him. But God creates situations for the development of our possibilities: the natural gifts we receive from God when we are born would depend on how we are going to use them. As the Russian singer Vladimir Vysotsky sang, "If you are dumb as a tree, you will be born a palm tree, and you will be a palm tree for a thousand years until you die." A problem is that people learn a lot but then don't put their new knowledge into practice. It is necessary to destroy this barrier and to start doing something after you've learned something. This practice is what life requires. Life demands a certain discipline. Life is an open energy and it needs to be released. With each century, the human ability to learn increases. If we decide that we know everything, our growth will come to an end.

I very much liked Leonardo's approach to illnesses—he believes it is possible to cure any illness through breath. And a person is strong enough to do it! One mistake of Western medicine and those who follow it is the tendency to focus only on the body; they forget about the soul. It is even possible to cure Down syndrome—it is just necessary to limit the space around such patients and they will recover. Everyone can be cured and transformed. It just depends on the amount of energy you are willing to spend. It is better to teach people how to cure themselves! Breath is one way of curing the body; it doesn't do any harm. Why hasn't anyone thought of this before? After all, we were born breathing! Why not use breathing according to its intended purpose?

Once Leonardo was late for a session. He looked tired and pinched, but was still smiling a lot. He told us that he was going to have a heart attack that morning but he just breathed it out. After a couple of hours, he was conducting our. That was the best demonstration of the power of breathing.

THE FOURTEENTH DAY.
REBIRTHING WITH IRINA

Thursday, March 27, 2008

We performed our morning respiratory gymnastics using a special technique: inhaling through the right nostril and exhaling through the left. Having closed the left nostril, we breathed through the right and exhaled the left, and so on. Such breath harmonizes chakras. We did four short connected inhalations and exhalations and then a long one—a full-blown completed breath through our lungs and thorax. And then free, silent breathing.

I came to the session to get rid of all the mess I had in my head—though at the time I didn't know this. During the session, I realized that I don't trust anybody and I do not feel my value. But I couldn't understand where all those thoughts were coming from. I had neither feelings nor desires—it was as though all my receptors were switched off and the machine had stopped working. I was breathing for thirty-five minutes, but nothing happened. I was just breathing. Pictures from my childhood gradually began to show up. There was my confident mother, who always knew what she wanted, and my always-doubting father, hardly able to make decisions. There I was, never saying what I wanted because my mom decided and did everything for me. Instead of being given a fishing rod and taught how to fish, the fish was already on my plate. And consequently, when I was growing up I thought that meat was extracted from dumplings. This is the other reason my first marriage was a failure: neither he nor I wanted to take responsibility and to work on our relationship. Instead, we began to copy our parents, and when it became absolutely intolerable, we simply pretended to be kids. Probably, my conscious mind couldn't stand so much truth and for twenty minutes I felt disconnected and fell into a meditative dream. Leaving it, I saw how a cloud the same size as my body rose up in me and left. After that, I started to breathe easily and freely. I was released from something that had been weighing upon me for a long time. My breath became even, and energy began to flow through my body like an electric current. But still at my temples and the third eye, it felt as if there were stoppers, and I wanted to pull out them physically. I began pulling them out but then felt a necessity to clear my whole head—I began tearing my hair out and swinging my head from side to side. Then I found my palms were removing a film from my eyes—I wanted to see a reality instead of the imagined world. But still, I felt that something was missing. Then I remembered what I wanted to work on during the session: trust and positive self-esteem. When I remembered, my internal voice pronounced it and a white column of light suddenly grew in me. I felt that I had my own boundaries and could see a hollow space in myself. And the voice told me that I hadn't trusted anybody because I never had a sense of myself and my boundaries. That's why any person could pass through me. And when people were living at my expense, I started to feel inconvenient, exploded with anger, undertook something. But eventually, I always felt guilty. And they just kept on using me. Everything repeated itself. It was always difficult for me to make decisions concerning my own life; it was easier for me to let someone else arrange things. It was the same with my free time—I preferred someone to plan my vacation for me rather than thinking of something on my own.

The voice continued to say that these boundaries would protect me like an alarm system. When you approach a car too closely, it itself feels human presence even though you're just passing it by and an alarm would be on. I understood that if you are afraid to walk, you can't move forward. But together with the ability to walk, our body possesses the mechanism which that us about possible dangers: we can see, hear, or feel an approaching obstacle or barrier. And we shouldn't be obsessed with this idea that there can be an obstacle somewhere, otherwise we won't move. And I felt this mechanism in myself. It hadn't been generated before, because in my childhood I everything was handed to me

The most interesting part of the session was that when we pulled out a Tarot card to explain what was happening to me, the myth about the goddess Ivannah had dropped out. In this myth, the young queen of the heavens, the morning and evening star, came to the earth, found a tree, and gave it the pleasure of life in hope to receive a throne and a bed. But one day she came to the tree, but it was occupied: there was a snake around its trunk, a bird in its leaves, and, the worst of all, Lilith, a dark power, had built herself a nest there. Ivannah began to cry and beg, but the gods refused to help her. Then a man called Gillonesh came and cut down a tree and made a throne and a bed out of it for Ivannah. Who is Lilith? In this history she symbolizes a dark side, a shade of Ivannah—her internal, material *I*. When we perceive our life as only light and pleasure, we do not only hide from reality, but we also limit our powers. Ivannah asked for a bed and a throne, but she did nothing to help herself. When Lilith stole her tree, Ivannah could only lament. Gillonesh had to rescue her. Therefore, the card points toward pain we received from something valuable in our lives, something that didn't happen the way we wanted it to.

But at the same time, the card asks us to look deep into ourselves and find the cause of our pain. What is it that frightens us? Which part of our power was rejected? It could be sorrow from something missing, an emotional pain, or a deep grief that overwhelms our soul. It is necessary to look for the source.

THE FIFTEENTH DAY.
BODY AND BRAIN

Friday, March 28, 2008

I woke up and felt a strong desire to run. It took me a while to understand where the desire to run came from—my brain or my body. If the body doesn't want to do something, the brain can't force it. When the body doesn't want to gather upand simply spreads inside, the brain can't control it. Therefore, I waited until my body responded and wanted something at last. Although the body lives on its own, it needs to be noticed and respected. While jogging, my body started to refuse to keep moving, but the brain chimed in. It was as though the brain shouted at the body, "keep on running!" It seemed like my feet existed separately from me and I couldn't even understand who I was, but was grateful for my brain's help. The pain resolved by itself, and I no longer needed to stop and rest. And there I felt the reality of managing your body and emotions! If you, having woken up in the morning, wonder how your left rib feels and whether it wants to wake up and go to the bathroom, believe me that without a doubt the answer will always be no. You will just spoil your mood and the morning will become gloomy! Stop asking! The rib isn't an organ—your desire is more important! A simple piece of advice: get out of bed as soon as you've opened your eyes! You'll wake up in the shower. Enjoy your awakening!

THE SIXTEENTH DAY.
REBIRTHING WITH ERIC

Saturday, March 29, 2008

Morning power gymnastics: we all stood in a circle, closed our eyes, and tried to feel what we were thinking—what our body and soul wanted. Then we opened our eyes, introduced ourselves, and started showing how we felt. During the gymnastics, I felt that my powers increased and I wanted to share mine with somebody. I expressed a desire to be a rebirther for Eric. The night before we were talking and he told me that he wanted to get to a new level of living, a new level of consciousnesses and sensation. Before the session I, as usual, asked what how he wanted to direct his thoughts before he started breathing. His throat had been sore for several days, so we decided to work with a throat chakra: it defines self-actualization and self-display in the world, i.e. the ability to say and do what you want.

Eric started to breathe. I felt and heard that his breath was very weak—there was no movement of energy in it. I suggested that he breathe through his mouth in order to lift the energy from his second chakra and push it out through the throat. His breath became intensive and strong, but not as powerful as I wanted. I started to move energy; I gave him some feedback and told him what he should visualize, and how he should learn to manage energy. The process went on intensively for thirty minutes, and then Eric left for the meditative dream connected with his fear of death and a necessity to take responsibility for his present life. I helped him for fifteen minutes, constantly pulling him toward consciousness, but he didn't want it. Then I energetically released him and began to read an affirmation (positive installation) as a mantra: "I, Eric, take responsibility for my life. I, Eric, can decide by myself how many years I'm going to live. I, Eric, am a strong and powerful person." I was waiting for him to make a decision. After some time, he began to breathe. It was a sign to me that he took responsibility for himself. When we were talking about what he saw during his breathwork session, he called me "a Russian military rebirther," meaning that he got a power "magic ass-kick". Buddha came to him and presented the Holy Grail. His reaction was quite calm—he just took what he was given.

THE SEVENTEENTH DAY.
A SESSION WITH IRINA

Monday, March 31, 2008

I came to the session with a strong desire to take responsibility for my life, to cease to regret my decisions, and to get rid of my parent syndrome concerning everything. A parent syndrome for me means being a Mum in any relationship, providing too much care and not sharing responsibilities with anyone, just doing everything by myself. I wanted to know what partnership really feels like because in my life I had learned to play only two roles: a good daughter and a good mother. All the men in my life—close relationships/friendships and even strangers—took advantage of me in some way. Some took my money and others lived at my expense. I realized that this was happening because of my parental instinct, which turned on every time someone needed something. I thought this was just fine, that these men just needed my help. But they took me for granted. And I continued to give and care about them, without realizing that I had this problem. For me, true partnership was something mysterious and unknown. From time to time, people suggested that I open a training center that focused on languages and spiritual practices. People were even ready to invest their money, but the thought that I would owe them blocked my oxygen. My perception of business boiled down to two roles: mother and child, boss and subordinate. The idea of partnership didn't exist for me at that time.

I started to breathe. As I found out later, I breathed only eight minutes and then left for a meditative dream that sucked me as a bog—viscous and warm. I heard Irina's voice, but I had no power to get out of the bog . . . and no desire. It was a very strong sweet dream, and I stayed there for an hour. A phrase, said in English, "God loves us all!" pulled me out of it. And I started to breathe again. I had a kaleidoscope of pictures in front of my eyes: my relatives, my boss at the university. As I wasn't breathing, there was nothing happening and I had a feeling of incompleteness and dissatisfaction. But I understood perfectly: if there is no work, there is no result. The point is that while breathing, a body accumulates a necessary amount of energy and provides our subconsciousness with the protection it needs in order to find the right solution for a problem. If problems lie on a surface, simple breathing will be enough for them to be resolved. The deeper and more dramatic a problem is, the more energy it will take to pull them out from the unconscious to the conscious level. And it will take more energy to understand and integrate it.

Probably, that's why a unicorn came to me for a consolation; I physically felt its horn in my third eye. A unicorn means cleanliness and divine blessing—the one who has the honor to see it receives enlightenment as though was visited by the Lord. Then there was a blue light, but it wasn't pure. It was dirty-gray, like a fog, and it also didn't bring a feeling of satisfaction to me because I didn't feel clarity. The Tarot card, Three Stones, which showed my process, Irina first dropped the Tarot card face down dropped face down, which meant dissatisfaction, especially in work, the inability to use potential for further developments, and the necessity of skill development. At the end of the breathing session, the same card was dropped in a direct position, which meant mastery, completeness, and success in work—also self-esteem and public acceptance, an ability to work with others.

THE EIGHTEENTH DAY.
DEVIL

Tuesday, April 1, 2008

That morning I woke up and wanted to cry out, *I love you, life!* I came to the session with a desire to continue studying my unconscious and to try to make a way through the fog of the unknown. Physically, I already felt ready. I started to breathe and, as I didn't want to fall in a meditative dream at once, I decided to begin with something not so tragic and began to think about my relatives. Images of my mum, my father, my brother passed in front of my eyes, but nothing clung and there was nothing to work on. Then I just began to breathe. And there in my consciousness the question emerged, *Who am I?* A simultaneously simple and difficult question. The question surprised me because I had been living a very spiritual life for eight years. But, on the other hand, what had I been doing with all these angels, deities? With the healing and other gifts I possessed? Can they be crammed in the capacity of human perception? Who am I: an angel or a human? If I'm both, then what should I do? Should I run to a monastery or a church? Should I hide from people and cultivate independence in myself? Or should I decide that my spiritual wanderings are the delirium of a sick imagination and learn to fall in love with human pleasures? Who am I? And with that question, I felt that I left my body. With the help of the will power I returned myself, having calmed unconscious that I wouldn't ask it this question anymore. After some time, I asked it again and started departing. So we, with my unconscious, were playing hide-and-seek, and then I decided to breathe. I was just breathing and doing nothing; I decided to get enough energy to protect my consciousness. That time I didn't work, didn't see, and feel anything. I was just breathing and thinking about my clients, who also sometimes were just breathing, not seeing or feeling anything, and thinking that it was just a waste of time. Most interesting that I felt Irina sitting next to me; I heard her saying: "Keep working!" But my unconscious was not ready yet. And I didn't want to sleep without realizing anything.

After forty minutes of such "rest," there was a picture with the baby who was born on third chakra (solar plexus level). I just saw it surrounded with sunlight. And then a strange sound appeared in my breast, thin and not so pure, as though at a descant. My breath completely turned into this sound and burst outside; the mouth opened, and the throat began to reproduce a child's crying but there were no tears or sensations of crying. Then the crying turned into some vocal "rags." I can't find another word to describe it; it was a howl of broken sounds. There was a feeling that a devil got into me and I was trying to exorcise it. I can tell you what I found out later. I shouted as if being slaughtered. Then I understood what "a bad voice" meant. My body was twisting along with the voice. The voice took any keys, from a squeal to a high-pitched whine. The only thing I was thinking about that time was people who were in the house. I felt sorry for them, as those sounds of mine were horrifying. When the last groan left me—it was about ten minutes later—my body stretched and filled with light through the second chakra. Thank God! On a Tarot card, which we pulled out to understand the process that had happened to me, we saw "Devil"—it characterizes the dark essence which lives in us. The one who pulls this card becomes the owner of a double force of darkness and light.

After the session, I went for a walk, looking at the sun, listening to the birds. By evening, I was completely restored.

THE NINETEENTH DAY.
I AM REBIRTHER FOR WILLOW

Wednesday, April 2, 2008

Willow—a forty-five-year-old woman of Cherokee descent. She was something in between an average shaman, a healer, and a psychotherapist. To work with a colleague like her is honorable, but it is both difficult and easy simultaneously—because you are in a full view.

I asked what problem she wanted to work on and, with surprise, she told me that she doubted her professionalism and feared she lacked competence. And I perfectly understood her as this was my problem too: accepting the healer within. It turned out that I was not alone and my problem wasn't unique. In Russia concepts like energy, rebirthing, and healing are new and obscure, but they are widely known in other parts of the world. So, I think, there will be a lot of work to do! Willow started breathing and my hands moved over her chakras. I saw how my fingers, without being given a signal from the brain, were moving the chakras apart, pulling something out of them, cleaning and splashing it on candle fire. Meanwhile there was a strong stream of energy in my body, and it was growing very hot. My real voice, passing through my consciousness, were speaking out loud to Willow that she was a strong, wise, confident woman and that she doesn't need to prove anything to anybody. After thirty minutes, Willow opened her dumbfounded eyes and, without saying anything, took off out of the room like a shot from a gun.

After a while, I was approached by the head of center, Peace, who asked me to do a session with her. I was puzzled because I didn't receive any feedback from Willow. Peace then said something to me which I managed to understand only the next day, "I can be helped only by a very spiritually strong person who will take my problem and solve it without my help." I didn't understand what Peace was talking about, but she continued to ask me how many years I had been curing and who taught me to work with chakras. When I realized that she was talking about my healing session with Willow that morning, and that I had performed cold chakra surgery, I was in shock. Had I really done all those things?

That evening Willow told me that during the session she had seen different situations from her school years, when she started to lose self-confidence and said that my convincing words, "you can be yourself," suddenly made her world simple and clear.

As for me, once again I concluded that it was all about the way you accept yourself internally, about your readiness for publicity and elegant PR, to borrow concepts from my other profession.

THE TWENTIETH DAY.
MY REBIRTHER—PEACE

Thursday, April 3, 2008

That morning when we had to choose a rebirther, I chose Peace— she was a professional and, moreover, she was then under the daily guidance of Leonardo. Besides, our three weeks were coming to an end, and I had only two days before my departure for New York. It was the best moment for me to take part in a session with her because, as my sensations showed, I had already gotten rid of all my basic problems, and it would be interesting to experience her professional technique now that I was in more of a position to observe. The point is that when you are the client, it is very difficult to understand the technique of to the person working with you. At that time, I felt strong enough to be in a stream myself and to track the actions of the rebirther at the same time. I started to breathe and felt that I was filling with the energy of love and light from the breath. It was a new sensation. Usually the process of rebirthing was a hard work for the body and lungs—the throat sometimes dried up, the nose sometimes grew congested, and some people experienced cramps throughout their bodies. That time, possibly, my body had already gone through all the negative physiology and was ready to be filled with energy and light. There were strong sensations in my breast—it felt like I was going to burst with love and happiness. Such sensations usually arise from an external source, from love for somebody else, for example. But that time, these sensations arose without an external reason. And I understood that it was the sensation of universal love. That moment I didn't have an opportunity to ponder what was given to me. But later, after my arrival in Moscow, when I started teaching Reiki and carrying out rebirthing sessions, my clients suddenly began to give me feedback about their experience of universal love during our sessions. Moreover,commentaries for all meditations were coming to me from above—I was simply pronouncing what was said to me.

While I was breathing and continued to fill with energy, my mother's prohibitions during my childhood appeared on the surface—all of them lumbered hard on me; I didn't have time to sort them out and integrate them. My consciousness refused to work under such pressure and I silently plunged into a meditative dream and stayed there about twenty minutes. Only the rebirther can tell the exact length of a dream and the breath of the client because during the session the client is in a state of altered consciousness and experiences time differently. Very often my clients, after an hour of rebirthing, say that they feel like it's been just ten minutes. These sensations prove that time can be stopped and that it is not constant.

My dream stopped when I saw an image of Leonardo come to me and illuminate me with a fire. He breathed energy into me that I needed so much. While I was in the dream, Peace was carrying out the process very tenderly and talking to me constantly. I really liked her calm and deep voice, and I didn't feel alone. A bright silver light appeared in front of me—Silver Angel came to me and introduced itself. I heard divine angelic choir. And then I was told that I was going to talk to them. I had already seen them, but I had never talked to them. It would be interesting to try. at that moment, I felt myself a pure conductor of divine energy and realized that I had received everything I had been asking for, and even more. So, the only thing I had to do was to materialize my knowledge and skills. Om Shanty!

THE TWENTY-FIRST DAY.
THE LAST DAY

Friday, April 4, 2008

That day I carried out a session with Peace. How touching and helpless a person looks when facing problems! And it doesn't matter what social level this person occupies. What a responsibility healers take upon themselves! I was shivering inside thinking about the responsibility I had: I really wanted to help this person. Not because of any particular reason, but because she was a little part of God on our earth. The problem of Peace was in her relationship with her mother as a child and her mother's subsequent disapproval during Peace's childhood. My God, it looked so familiar to me! Why are all human problems so similar? She started to breathe, and tears were streaming down her cheeks. I started to move her energy so that she could cope with it. I talked to her and I asked her to forgive and release her mum, who had been young and inexperienced at that time. I asked her to use all the wisdom and experience of present-day Peace, a fifty-year old woman who had brought up two sons. All of us have the right to be mistaken, and the social status of the parent doesn't automatically make us wise and tolerant. When I was clearing Peace's chakras, her breathing grew a bit confused, but I asked her to continue. With persuasion, tears, and struggle, the calm gradually came, and I saw how the skin on her face smoothed and her breathing grew more even . . . After this session, Peace told me that she had seen me take each chakra, one at a time, and cut it, clean it, fill it with light, before closing and returning it. Miracles!

PART II

Now I have my ESOLANG spiritual center in Moscow and carry out rebirthing trainings on my own, and I share the the training you received there and. I have asked my clients to write on a forum of my website (www.esolang.com) what would be important for them to know before the first session of rebirthing. All comments are very sincere. And it is very pleasant to read these comments, as it is always desirable to get the impression and response from participants of the process. I hope their experience will help you to come to rebirthing, to solve your problems, and to discover new possibilities.

RESPONSES FROM REBIRTHING GROUP

Lena Myshkin (a lawyer; age 34):

When I came to breathe, there was a goal to breathe the problems out. What were my problems? I plainly couldn't formulate them at that time, and even now I do not understand them completely. I didn't know anything about rebirthing. I do not remember goals for each session now. Some come to mind, but, I think if I remember them it means that they are not breathed out to the end and would still bother me. Let me tell you a little about the physical sensations: it was difficult to breathe, there were tormented spasms, but soon, when the difficult work was done, there was an ease. However, I was frightened by the first session. I think, before rebirthing I should have learned more details about the possibility of negative feelings, as well as the importance of my physical condition (people with cardiovascular and pulmonary diseases should be aware of it either). Personally, I think that there is still a lot work to do. But one problem is that I don't want to breathe. On the whole, I didn't analyze the changes that have appeared after rebirthing and Reiki (I cannot tell what has affected what), but soon it will be a year since I've used migraine medication. Overall, I've become more confident, and I have some interesting career opportunities. I don't think up problems for myself anymore as I did earlier, and I hope for the best! Though, I still feel like I'm not doing anything important.

Anna Holina (marketing manager; age 21):

What would you like to know before rebirthing? For me, it would have been better to know more details about the possible physical reactions, about all the possible things that can occur in the body. Also, it would have been good to know about sounds that you hear during the session. That way, the one who is breathing would pay less attention to someone else's sounds, like complaining or crying. I think that that people should be warned that the sounds could be uncontrollable, and that they shouldn't be afraid of the sounds their body makes, or the sounds they hear from another body. Basically, it is necessary not to be afraid of anything. Personally, I was frightened, especially during the first session. My heart sank to my boots because of everything that was happening to my body and how it was physically reacting. And the most important thing: I was afraid that I wasn't able to control these processes! To me it was terrible because my body wasn't obeying me; I lost control of it completely! And sometimes when my crooked fingers or palms and wrists were rising, I wanted to lower them down or straighten them, but I simply couldn't do it! It was like it wasn't my body, like I tried to straighten somebody else's fingers. And once, during the sessions my spirit left my body! And the thought that came to my mind was: what if the session ends and I'm not back to my body? What should I do then? And the most ridiculous thought was: what will they say to my parents? In that moment I didn't feel either my own body, or the space around me. All those emotions and sensations you experience during a rebirthing session simply can't be described. You should try it yourself.

What goals were set? What have we got from rebirthing? I came to rebirthing with specific problems. There were a lot of them and I knew it. But as turned out, there were even more. Those hidden problems, which I wasn't aware of before, were revealed after a couple of sessions. My goal was quite clear: to get rid of all the garbage in my head and to solve problems. These were different problems than the others—they were both personal and professional. I had problems communicating with other people, as well as other complexes and fears. But the greatest problem was in me, in my way of thinking, in my consciousness. I was the biggest unresolved problem. I was ready, psychologically and morally, for this training and was hoping for the best future and a new life with my new "I." I knew there was a huge amount of work ahead of me, and I was ready for it, but my body obviously wasn't because during each session it overcame terrible transformations! All my problems were coming out through the physical reactions of my body. I was crying, complaining, rattling. My hands were crooked, half of my face was numb, there were cramps in my legs. Once, the bottom part of my face grew so numb that I could barely breathe! It was horrible! The only thing that kept me going was the knowledge that there was a teacher nearby and that everything was under control. I knew that if something went wrong, the teacher would be there to rescue me. Therefore, I simply immersed myself in this process.

Certainly, it is necessary to tell people about the special mental sensations. When the session ends, in the moment of relaxation after the hard work of breathing through problems, the consciousness absolutely changes. After such moments, I began to understand the meaning of the words "the changed condition of consciousness." You can't explain it. It's the same way that it's impossible to describe a color and to explain, say, to the blind person what is blue, or pink, or red, or yellow. These are inexpressible experiences and impressions.

Thanks to all the work of this rebirthing course, my life has really changed. I think that first of all, all changes were connected with one primary source: the change in my consciousness. When I changed myself, everything that surrounded me changed too! The most important thing is that my mentality and reactions to everything have changed. I, so to say, became wiser. My emotions and decisions became more deliberate—nervousness and impulsiveness have disappeared. Actually, I noticed positive changes in thinking after each session, but I felt the full effect after the end of the training. Now the knowledge that I received, all these breathing techniques, help me in everyday life. They help me to cope with my problems and difficulties, stresses, negative emotions, and fears. I am extremely grateful to my teacher and master, Inga Korjagina! Thanks for this invaluable and priceless gift, for her guidance, and for the fact that the negative things have left my life forever!

Alina (student; age 19):

When I first attended the training, I wanted to get rid of the mess inside me: the odd thoughts, fears, and my self-consciousness. Before the training, you really should know what happens with the physics of your body. I was scared when my arms were twisted. I got frightened and thought, that's it, I'll be crooked until the end of time. Then the uncontrollable emotions began. I was laughing as I never did before and then suddenly I was crying. It's strange when before the training you are told that you'll need to breathe about forty minutes. Why does it take so long? But right after the training you feel lightness in your body. If you feel this lightness, it means that something bad is gone. When you try to breathe some problem out, you understand how it's solved, but if you still feel fear it means you should keep on trying. Sometimes blocks are removed and you don't even know it. And then after some time, you realize that some of your worst fears have vanished. Inga, thank you! It's the vital energy of pure light.

Malika (CFO; age 28):

I would like to share my feelings right after the first rebirthing session. To me, these trainings were very opportune. I felt, physically, the need to regenerate my emotions, thoughts, and consciousness. During the first session I thought that I was either going to die or pass out. My reaction was very strong: a wild headache, nausea, dizziness, etc. Inga helps very much with the breath techniques; she breathes along with you! It helped me breathe such feelings up at once instead of leaving it until later. Now the plot thickens! Internal processes began to intensify; answers came by themselves; new creative abilities and needs opened. The first week I didn't have any physical strength to get up—all I wanted was to eat and sleep! The second week, I felt sick, but really my body was undergoing a cleansing. The training helped to remove these symptoms and to accelerate processes; it is proved by many people. An emotional condition during this period is unstable, but new feelings and desires appear. I only finished the training yesterday, so it's difficult to conclude right now . . . To be continued!

Inessa (MGIMO graduate; age 21):

I would love to share my feelings with you! Today I had the first session in the group rebirthing, and it was something indescribable! There are a lot of emotions and realizations! I am in shock! Many people say that during the sessions their bodies grow so stiff that it is impossible to move a limb. I didn't experience anything like that—my body reacted rather quietly. The only thing I felt was an ache in the shoulders—that's the thing I'm actually working on. I have realized that my relationships with my mum are the root of absolutely all my main worries and despondency. I didn't expect that I would burst into tears, though I heard from others that such things happen. I have almost finished an individual course, but never had such strong, deliberate emotions. Probably everything is about the difference in how you breathe—through the nose or through the mouth. Or maybe everything I studied before wasn't very in-depth, and only now this main worry has shown up and is ready to disappear. Anyway my feelings are unusual, and I'm looking forward to the next training!

Anna (IT specialist; age 30):

The first cycle of rebirthing training was hard work for me. Each session I had to put myself together and solve a problem regardless of internal resistance, and at the end of the session I felt ease, lightness, and happiness after I discovered the solution. With each new session there was a new problem, and much hard work! During the second cycle of rebirthing, I learned how to solve problems easily and with pleasure—the breathing was easy and pleasant. After the second rebirthing session I solved three big problems that I had been suffering from many years, not knowing what to do with them. One problem disappeared during the rebirthing session; the other two were resolved within one and a half months.

RESPONSES ABOUT
THE INDIVIDUAL REBIRTHING

Here are the responses of people who have had ten sessions of individual rebirthing. Some of them were in group rebirthing before and have compared both types of breathing.

Inessa (MGIMO graduate; age 21):

Yes, you should really try rebirthing! It was absolutely amazing! I can't find the appropriate words to describe my experiences! It's been about a month since I started exercising with Inga, but it seems like it was so long ago. And even now, when the cycle is over, I realize that there are still so many interesting things to do. But it's just a new level of perception, comprehension, and even living. The advantage of individual training, in my opinion, is that it's very delicate and careful. Well, I felt this way. To me, with all the muddle in my head, it would be impossible to start practicing rebirthing in a group, where, first of all, the other technique is used, and there is not much personal assistance from the teacher. Now that I practice rebirthing in a group, I can compare these two approaches to training. During the individual training Inga helps very much; she literally feels your worries and feelings. The technique, which is used during the individual trainings, helps you to breathe out any discomfort or physical/emotional sensations very easily, although everything is completely individualized. If it gets too hard, Inga is always there and cautious about what is going on. The consciousness clears, you become calmer—all the fuss and emotional stress are gone. This training is very pleasant. Of course, you'll have purification of your mind, thoughts and actions and this will be demonstrated in different situations, but it's necessary to remember that it's an inevitable stage: before you get to the next level, you have to get rid of everything you had before. And it isn't always pleasant, but it's worth it!

Kseniya (HR manager; age 28):

I've just had only one individual session, but I'll share my experience. Previously I had two rebirthing trainings in a group. The first time, I felt and saw almost nothing. I remember some bright fragments from the second time. It was difficult to breathe. Something made me come to an individual training, although I had doubts about it until the last second. It was easier to breathe; the technique is different. It was striking to hear that there was no time limit—we could breathe as long as we needed it. I got very useful recommendations that surprised me. Now the only thing doubts I have are the questions I need to work out in rebirthing."

Zuliya (manager; age 30):

Yesterday I had my first session of training. When I was going there, I had no idea about rebirthing. I thought Inga would show me some technique to breathe well. When everything started, my biggest problem came out—the thing I fear the most. This fear paralyzed me and didn't let me be myself. I could neither inhale nor exhale. Inga helped me, and I could breathe again. The problem started to let up, and, for the first time in my life, I departed from my body. This is difficult to describe, but my dream now is to learn how to meditate and get to this state on my own. I can't wait for the next session. Thank you, master!

Anna (IT specialist; age 30):

I've just completed the individual rebirthing course. The last two sessions summed up all the work I had done; I became wiser. I created the image and form for my life. I stopped dashing and hanging about. I know my goals and what potential I have to achieve them. I know what I live for and where I'm going. Inga, thank you very much!

Oksana (housewife, mother of two children; age 36):

When I first came to Inga I was depressed and felt like I was in a deadlock. "How am I going to live on? I didn't have the strength or desire to analyze the problems that had led me to that state of absolute darkness. After the first session, Inga removed the block, and when I breathed out my problem, I was able to look at it from another point of view and came up with a solution. It was just that simple! With every session, I grew calmer, more confident, and full of energy and willpower. Another pleasure was to be near such a nice and clever person like Inga! We had no problems communicating! This was very unusual for me, as I'm not very sociable. After the course of individual rebirthing, I feel renewed and, moreover, now I do know how I'm going to live on. I'm sure that I'll solve all my problems. I never felt so strong and determined. And one thing more—I'm very happy! Inga, thank you very much!

DEAR READER,

Having read this book, you probably also want to make the fascinating journey deep into yourselves. For those who feel something more in themselves but don't dare to admit it, you might be interesting to know more about my trainings—my spiritual and healing programs where I train people to be wizards of their lives, to be independent and whole-hearted.

You can find more about me, and my services, on my website: www.esolang.com.

Here are some descriptions of my trainings.

REIKI

Reiki is a name for the salutary energy that is in nature. To be engaged with Reiki, no magic is required because laying hands on the body of a person or an animal, to console or relieve a pain, is an ancient phenomenon.

Reiki is present in us initially. Some researchers of Reiki say that it was included in our genetic code as the congenital right of all people.

The adjustment process, or dedication, distinguishes Reiki from all other forms of laying on hands or touch healing. Adjustment, or initiation, is not a healing session; it makes you a healer increasing positive power of a human ability to transfer the energy through him. After the initiation, the power stream is felt in the hands, and is experienced through various sensations of heat, pricking, and vibrations. And then you can feel your healing abilities.

The person who practices Reiki doesn't create the energy by himself but is simply the channel for its transferring; Reiki itself is the thing that heals.

Reiki is harmless and operates through clothes and distance.

Reiki intensifies the creative potential and energy of a person. It improves memory and creates a positive spirit, helps a person to overcome rage and fear, and to live in peace and harmony with the world around.

REBIRTHING BY THE LEONARDO ORR TECHNIQUE

The conscious breath, or rebirthing, was discovered by Leonardo Orr in the 1970s. Since then, it has become very popular technique in both personal problem-solving and addiction. You can clear your mind, your body, your heart and soul, and also increase your vital activity and personal interest to live for your soul.

Rebirthing is an open an easy way to be filled with divine energy. According to L. Orr, rebirthing is biological knowledge of God.

Realize and cure eight big obstacles: birth trauma, the syndrome of parental disapproval, negative thinking or installations, unconscious fear of death, school trauma, memory loss (temporary or age-specific), social trauma (building of communism and party installations), violence, and problems of past lives.

Open the spiritual practices which you can easily apply in your daily life.

Feel deep communication with yourself and forces to cure problems in your relations with people.

The conscious breath, rebirthing, is perhaps the most valuable self-curing technique which we can learn!

My know-how: I support the energy of breath and can perform operations on chakras if the client is unable to cope with a problem through breath alone. I remove the blocks by myself.

ANGELIC HEALING

Have you ever talked to your angels? Even if you haven't, you've always felt the presence of somebody and something unknown in your space. Intuitively, you always felt that there was also another world besides the material one, but nobody wanted to listen to you. Now you're not alone! If you want to meet with people just like you and to learn your higher mission on this earth and in this incarnation, this training is for you.

Angelic energy is very soft and unostentatious. Any sensitive person can feel it. But through this training, angels will begin to help you deliberately. You will learn how to manage situations and your life, how to heal yourselves, your relatives, and friends with the help of angelic support.

In the course of training you will learn:

o To increase your intuitive abilities
o To read a person's aura
o To read and interpret angelic cards
o To receive messages from your angels
o To communicate with your guardian angel and those of your relatives and clients
o To work with the energy of money
o To be released from dependencies (smoking, alcohol)

o   To build relationships with your beloved and children

o   To work with light energy

And also you will:

o   feel angelic ease and tirelessness

o   learn your vital mission

o   believe in yourself!

HEALING BY SOUND OR THE SOUND OF YOUR BODY

Can you listen to your body? And can you hear it? It's alive and wants to tell you about itself. It wants to help you to blossom and feel like a fragrant flower, shining in tender rays of sunlight and fresh morning dew . . .

You've never treated your body this way? Did you torture it by keeping it within the bounds of society, family, and confined spaces? But it's alive and waiting for you to listen to it.

First level of training will help you to:

o   discover your genuine sound and voice

o   fill and relax your body with the help of sound

o   listen to and hear your body

o   heal your body and cellular memory

o   read the information with the help of sound

Second level of training will help you to:

o   heal others with the help of sound

MEDITATIVE DRAWING

This training is aimed at immersing yourself in your own, hidden or scarcely shown, talents and abilities, and learning how to trust yourself. Simultaneously balancing your right (emotional) and left (logical) hemispheres, you'll get rid of nervousness, excitement, fear, unwillingness, and laziness. Internal barriers will fall away by themselves.

Languages, which the left hemisphere is responsible for, become easily accessible and fluid. You'll discover new potential and feel sensations of pleasure and happiness.

In the course of discussion, a person learns to defend his opinion, choosing whether to accept something or not, and becomes complete and independent of others' opinions.

The techniques of potential disclosing through drawing are also called art therapy because sometimes it's easier to draw something than to explain it. Therefore, it is very important to learn to understand the things that we reveal on paper.

REBIRTHING. LESSONS ABOUT THE CONSCIOUS BREATH

Marina (manager; age 32):

Inga! I was very glad to see you, and many thanks for the book.

After the meeting, I came home with the thought that I need to tidy up the apartment a little bit. Well, I thought, I'll read a page and do some cleaning. A page wasn't enough! I've already finished reading. It's very easy and interesting to read this book!

My first thought was: "Do things like that really happen? It is all true?" Even the situation with the fire seemed a fairytale, let alone the rebirthing sessions! And, as I also said, I kind of believe, but at the same time I think that it's impossible with me . . . that with the help of breathing, you can get rid of so many problems and fears . . . I think I would like to try it . . . I have many fears: fear of my husband, that once again he won't understand, that there will be some misunderstanding, a conflict; fear of the reaction of my body and soul; fear of the unknown, whether things will work out. Well, there are a lot of things to work on. And the most interesting thing is that when, two years ago, I was looking for an English tutor and there were many offers, I stumbled across you! After all, there was something behind that. I understood it at once, during the first lesson when you carried out the first meditation. But then I tried to forget everything and just study the language. Once again, thanks for the book! Thanks for agreeing to meet and for giving it to me!!!

Now I'm dreaming about a continuation, or about a series of books. And it would be great if they could last longer. In whole, you made it!

Anna (marketing expert; age 21):

I've read the book. I like it very much! Many thanks!

Katerina (marketing manager; age 24):

Inga! It's impossible to stop reading this book! With the help of it, those who still have some doubts or don't understand something will have an opportunity to make a final decision! My congratulations!!!

Malika (CFO; age 28):

Inga, my compliments! The thing you feel after finishing the book is a desire to understand, to comprehend. I have so many questions . . . I would also want to get more details about some sessions. The descriptions are thorough, but it seems like many things here are intentionally left out.

Elena (numerologist; age 45):

Inga, thank you for the book and the frankness in it!

Lilya (manager; age 35):

I've read this book with a great pleasure. After having finished it everyone asks himself—Who am I? What I was born for? How do I live on? How can I be happy? And of course, you want to find a person who knows the answers to these questions but doesn't require a life of isolation without creature comforts. This book is written by such person who has transformed into a leader. The unusual experiences and internal transformations described in this book are very absorbing. However, it's also an opportunity to find those key words that will awaken the sleeping consciousness and create a desire to regenerate yourself and work for your future. Thank you!